C000138715

DOG WAITING

PHOTOGRAPHS BY **LISA VANDY**

BOXTREE

First published 2007 by Boxtree
an imprint of Pan Macmillan Publishers Ltd
Pan Macmillan, 20 New Wharf Road, London N1 9RR
Basingstoke and Oxford
Associated companies throughout the world
www.panmacmillan.com

ISBN-13: 978-0752-22630-9
ISBN-10: 0-7522-2630-4

Copyright © 2007 Here+There World Ltd
Photographs Copyright © 2007 Lisa Vandy
  except page 50, © 2007 Lily Richards;
  pages 72-73, © 2007 Ben Mangham;
  pages 86-87, © 2007 Sarah Shackleton

Design: Caz Hildebrand

9 8 7 6 5 4 3 2 1

A CIP catalogue record for this book is
available from the British Library.

Printed in China by Imago

For Daphne Vandy and Valerie Govan

INTRODUCTION

The sight of a dog waiting for its owner is often moving; the poignancy of the dog's expression can, it's true, be comical, but it can also be heart-breaking. The act of being tied up outside a shop can occur for some dogs every morning, yet their anxiety levels still remain the same.

I started taking these pictures for my own enjoyment, but I soon realised that the pathos I captured in my photographs had a universal appeal and that I'm not alone in empathising with waiting dogs. Perhaps we find it easy to identify with the dogs' fear of abandonment? Often the dogs I encountered were being greeted by passersby of all ages, people who stroked the dogs, chatted to them, perhaps trying to reassure them that they won't be left there for ever, alone.

After all, as happy as the dogs are to meet new people, they are all, basically, only waiting, often anxiously, for one person...

New York, USA

Lucy, Burnham Market, Norfolk

Max, Dalston, London

Jessie, Totnes, Devon

Warsaw, Poland

Hackney, London

Golborne Road, London

Blackie, Aldeburgh, Suffolk

Molly Tuck, Burnham Market, Norfolk

Ralph, Gospel Oak, London

Lollipop, Primrose Hill, London

Lollipop, Primrose Hill, London

Flash, Stamford Hill, London

Molly, Highbury Corner, London

Lolie, Hackney, London

Stoke Newington, London

Hackney, London

Tilly, Hayling Island, Hampshire

Tansy, Hayling Island, Hampshire

Pickles, Hackney, London

Jack and Duchie,
Hackney, London

Heather, Hackney, London

Hackney, London

Mel and Lua, New York, USA

Totnes, Devon

Ice, Hornsey, London

Oscar and Rosie, Hayling Island, Hampshire

Hackney, London

Gwillam, Aldeburgh, Suffolk

Stoke Newington, London

Marylebone, London

Belsize Park, London

Dolly, Hackney, London

Lucy, Stoke Newington, London

Scrabble, Primrose Hill, London

Aldeburgh, Suffolk

Stoke Newington, London

Burnham Market, Norfolk

Chiswick, London

Leftie, Highgate, London

Jess, Aldeburgh, Suffolk

Totnes, Devon

Hackney, London

South End Green, London

Ling, Aldeburgh, Suffolk

Gerrard, Katonah, USA

Yoda, Knightsbridge, London

Lucy, Marylebone, London

Tinkerbell, Totnes, Devon

Dylan, Stoke Newington, London

Name, Location

Nellie, Columbia Road, London

Walberswick, Suffolk

Patsy, Budleigh Salterton, Devon

Beth, Acton, London

Chloe, Totnes, Devon

Venice, Hackney, London

Spock, Bigbury, Devon

Exeter, Devon

Aldeburgh, Suffolk

Tara, Stamford Hill, London

Shadow and Poppy, Budleigh Salterton, Devon

Dotty, Stoke Newington, London

Fizz, Budleigh Salterton, Devon

Emma and Lucy, Aldeburgh, Suffolk

Barney, Twickenham, Middlesex

Ruby, Totnes, Devon

Aur, Aria and Kim, Totnes, Devon

Buzz, Los Angeles, USA

Buzz, Los Angeles, USA

Bobby, Totnes, Devon

Milo, Stoke Newington, London

Digby, Budleigh Salterton, Devon

Betty and Flash, Dalston, London

Molly, Chingford, Essex

Glory and Foo, Shoreditch, London

Max, Totnes, Devon

Sherry, Coffee and Shula, Budleigh Salterton, Devon

Zoe, Budleigh Salterton, Devon